GOD'S
A True Story of Brave Faith in Ethiopia
CHILD

Written and Illustrated by
Justine Taylor

God's Child: A True Story of Brave Faith in Ethiopia
Text and Illustrations © 2025 by Justine Taylor. All Rights Reserved.

No part of this book may be reproduced, stored in a retrieval system, or transmitted in any form or by any means—electronic, mechanical, photocopy, recording, or otherwise—without prior written permission from the publisher, except brief quotations used in connection with reviews. This manuscript may not be entered into AI, even for AI training. For permission, email permissions@wclbooks.com.

Mission Kids is an imprint of William Carey Publishing (WCP). These books are designed for young readers to nurture a passion for the peoples of the world and inspire them to participate in God's global mission. The stories and ideas in this book reflect the author's perspective and experiences and may not represent the views of the publisher.

William Carey Publishing (www.missionbooks.org) is a ministry of Frontier Ventures, Pasadena, CA (www.frontierventures.org)

All Scripture quotations, unless otherwise indicated, are taken from the ESV® Bible (The Holy Bible, English Standard Version®), Copyright © 2001 by Crossway, a publishing ministry of Good News Publishers. Used by permission. All rights reserved.

Scripture quotations marked NIV are taken from the Holy Bible, New International Version®, NIV®. Copyright © 1973, 1978, 1984, 2011 by Biblica, Inc.™ Used by permission of Zondervan. All rights reserved worldwide. www.zondervan.com. The "NIV" and "New International Version" are trademarks registered in the United States Patent and Trademark Office by Biblica, Inc.™

Scripture quotations marked NLT are taken from the Holy Bible, New Living Translation, copyright ©1996, 2004, 2015 by Tyndale House Foundation. Used by permission of Tyndale House Publishers, Carol Stream, Illinois 60188. All rights reserved.

Cover Illustration: Justine Taylor
Cover and Interior Designer: Mike Riester

ISBNs: 978-1-64508-648-2 (paperback)
       978-1-64508-704-5 (epub)

Printed Worldwide

29 28 27 26 25   1 2 3 4 5   IN

Library of Congress Control Number: 2025944333

A Note to Parents and Teachers

This book deals with some heavy themes like communism, war, torture, illness, and death. I've tried to explain these ideas in ways that are suitable for children, but please consider reading and discussing this book with them.

*Ethiopia is a country in the eastern part
of the continent of Africa.*

For Chris,

You've taught me countless things, and one of them is how to dream big. Writing this story was your idea. I am continually the joyful and terrified beneficiary of your big ideas.

Contents

Introduction	1
1. God's Child	3
2. Revolution!	23
3. Love and Terror	47
4. Ready to Die and Free to Live	65
5. The Finish Line	85
Epilogue	111
Acknowledgments	115

Introduction

Dear Reader, do you think you can be sad *and* joyful at the same time? Do you think you can be in pain, *and* also have peace? Can a situation be very hard, *and* be very good?

Let me tell you a true story that shows these things can be so. The story is at times frightening and heartbreaking, yet it is full of beauty and glory. The wise person knows that these kinds of stories are important for our hearts. They can give us courage for whatever we may face, knowing that God has been faithful, and he will be again.

1

God's Child

Come with me to Ethiopia. Journey between the rocky green highlands in the north and the parched deserts of the south. Let us go far from the bustling streets of the capital city, Addis Ababa, and walk down rutted dirt roads. These roads are clouded with dust, kicked up by overloaded buses hurtling past.

We'll go into the small town of Wolisso, through its marketplace. Take a deep breath. It is fragrant from the amber mounds of spices for sale. But watch your step! Clucking chickens skitter underfoot, and they will scold you! Look at the hills. Cattle lower their heavy horns to graze on the dry grass slopes.

Keep going until you see a little house. This house sits in the middle of tall enset trees. The trees stretch up to the sun while giving cool shade beneath.

God's Child

The house is circular, with a shaggy thatched roof that covers much of the home. In the yard, a garden plot features tall cornstalks. Nearby, a few naughty-looking goats wander, looking for trouble. Inside the house is a little baby with a big smile, who was born in the early 1950s. This baby has a remarkable story, which you will discover if you keep reading.

Negussie was born in a house like this one.

The baby's name was Negussie Kumbi. The name might sound odd. This is partly because many of you don't speak Amharic, which is the main language in Ethiopia. But when you learn what it means, it will make even less sense. Negussie means "My King." How could this little baby, born in a poor home in the backcountry of Ethiopia, have any royal heritage? And while the baby's name carried such honor and promise, the truth was that others would soon reject him.

In those days, and in that area, sometimes a man would have several wives. This isn't God's good plan for marriage. From the beginning, God said a man should stay close to his wife. Only two people should unite as one (Genesis 2:24).

But a lot of people in Ethiopia did not know or follow God. Many people called themselves "Orthodox Christians." Since ancient times, some of them drifted from key teachings of the Bible. As they moved further away, their faith changed beyond recognition. The good news of salvation in Jesus was forgotten and changed.

Even more, many people in Ethiopia still followed old local religions. They believed in strong, evil spirits that need to be appeased. They lived in fear and followed the burdensome rules set by witch doctors. And this was true of Negussie's family. They were a little bit of Orthodox, a little bit of local spiritism, and almost none of the one true God.

Negussie's father was from one tribe of people, and his mother was from another tribe. This was unusual because these two groups often didn't like each other and definitely wouldn't marry each other. Negussie's father also had another wife, who lived in a different house on a different little farm.

As Negussie started to grow, it became clear that he was not a healthy boy. He didn't appear to be developing properly. His back was short and hunched over, and he was very small for his age. Perhaps, you may think, they should have gone to a hospital, or seen a doctor or therapist to find out what was wrong? But the superstitious beliefs about evil spirits made them afraid to visit nearby hospitals or clinics run by Christian missionaries.

Instead, as a small child, his mother decided to give Negussie away. What help could a small, weak, deformed boy be to her? Maybe she was disappointed or maybe she was overwhelmed. We do not know. As a little boy, he was sent to live with his father's other wife. She was unhappy about getting a child who wasn't hers. He was the son of a rival woman from another ethnic group. She also saw Negussie's bent little body and decided that he would not be useful to have around.

This is a sad beginning to our story. For a mother to reject her child is one of the most heartbreaking things in the world. It is unfair and shortsighted to despise a little boy because of a disability. And to hate someone because of the people group they come from is wrong and foolish.

God's heart is *for* people who are different or weak. He loves each person in this world. He created us in his own image! He wants us to be like him. We should love and care for those who are different, weak, or disabled. He has shown us this same care in our own weakness. And even more, God has proved over and over that our weakness, when it is in his hands, can bring great glory.

God's Child

With this sad start to his life, could God still use Negussie to do amazing things? Yes! Even if his back was stunted and bent? Yes! Did God make Negussie to be born out of two ethnic groups who didn't get along for a reason? Yes! God, as he always does, used this sad beginning for very good reasons.

Because Negussie's stepmother didn't like to have him around the house, she would shoo him outside. There, he would sit on a small stool by the gate and enjoy the sunshine. That turned out to be just the place God wanted him to be.

Negussie had a beautiful smile and twinkling eyes!

Let me tell you another important detail about Negussie. Despite facing tough times, feeling lonely, and having a sickly body, he had a radiant smile. A big, broad, beautiful smile with eyes that twinkled! And behind that smile, he had a heart that often looked for the good things instead of thinking only of the bad things.

One day, as Negussie sat alone, enjoying the warmth of the sun, a lady walked by and saw this small boy with the shining smile. This lady was a missionary nurse named Betty Martin.

Betty and others like her left their home countries to tell the people of Ethiopia the good news of Jesus. These missionaries also set up clinics and hospitals, schools and churches. They learned the languages and lived among the different people groups in cities or villages. They searched for ways to help and connect with people. They wanted to teach them about the only path to salvation—Jesus Christ's death and resurrection.

Right next to Negussie's stepmother's home was a station where some missionaries lived and worked. It was a group of buildings with a school, clinic, church, and homes for missionaries to live in. It was called "Obi."

Betty worked at the Obi mission station. When she saw Negussie's crumpled body as she walked by, she wondered what had happened to him to make him that way. She wanted to speak to his parents about getting the medical help the boy needed. But no parent was in sight. She asked the little boy, "Whose child are you?"

The little boy beamed up at her and responded, "I'm God's child."

In the Bible, it tells us that to all who receive Jesus by believing in his name, he gives the right to become children of God (John 1:12). At this point, Negussie had not learned about Jesus. This little boy, rejected by his birth mother and not accepted by his stepmother, felt he must belong to someone. Somehow, he knew deep in his heart that there was a God out there—one who had made him and the world around him. So, he concluded, he must belong to God. This was a God he did not yet know, but he believed that God was there.

God's Child

His answer surprised the nurse. She knew it was true that God created and loved this child. Negussie was right, even if he didn't understand how incredible his answer was.

As she spoke to him, her eyes studied his form. Her mind reviewed the medical knowledge she had studied at school and obtained in her time as a nurse. She thought Negussie had a certain kind of tuberculosis. This disease had affected his spine. It could get worse, leading to leg paralysis or even death. But a doctor could treat it with medicine.

It was too late to fix his back, but the medicine could stop the disease from getting worse. She asked Negussie's parents again and again if he could go to a hospital for treatment, but they would not agree to it. They worried about upsetting the spirits they believed controlled their lives. They were also suspicious of the missionaries, who weren't part of the old Ethiopian Orthodox church.

Finally, though, Nurse Betty prevailed, and they allowed him to go away to a clinic for treatment. Negussie received the medical care he needed.

He returned home healthy, but he was still bent from the damage the disease had already caused.

Negussie spent a lot of time at Obi Station.

Now that Betty knew Negussie and knew that his health was improving, she invited him to attend the Obi Station elementary school. There he could learn reading, writing, and mathematics, and learn to speak English. Negussie's life began sadly when he was sent away from his mother. However, God did wonderful things for him. Because he had moved away from his first home, he now lived close to Obi

Station. He received the medical care he needed, and he gained access to educational opportunities. But God's blessings were not done. Soon, God would send Negussie a family who loved him.

One day, Negussie peeked into the Obi yard. He saw people gathering, smiling, and shaking hands. He saw faces he did not recognize. It seemed to be a family with three children, each with sandy-blonde hair glinting in the sunlight. Negussie saw a boy who was about his size. The boy looked a bit younger, as Negussie was small for his age. The boy had a shy smile and ears that stuck out stubbornly beneath his neatly combed hair.

Negussie soon learned that a new missionary family had moved from the big city of Addis Ababa to the little Obi Station in the countryside. Bea and Murray Coleman came to this mission station in central Ethiopia. They wanted to learn the languages and culture. They also hoped to befriend and love the Ethiopian people whom their Lord loved first. They wanted to share the great news of knowing and following Jesus with their new neighbors. The Colemans were from Canada, but in a short time, Ethiopia became their beloved home.

The boy with the sandy-blonde hair and ears that stuck out was their son, John. Since most of you speak English, you may be familiar with the name "John." Do you know what it means? It means "God is gracious." That name may make more sense to you than Negussie's. God *is* gracious. He shows us his love even when we don't deserve it. He is kind and merciful to us.

Negussie gained a best friend.

But as our story goes on, both John and Negussie may have wondered—*is* God really gracious? They would face some terrible, scary, upsetting things in the future. But let me tell you—it *is* always true. Even when we go through the hardest times in our lives, God is still gracious. He is always good and always loving, even in situations we don't like or understand.

Even though John was a few years younger than Negussie, they became best friends. They would climb the big sprawling tree in the middle of the Obi yard. They would venture off into the woods where Negussie taught John how to find the colorful, unique Ethiopian birds that fascinated John. Each new bird felt like a jewel from lost treasure for John to discover. He was in awe of Negussie's ability to find them. They splashed in the river on hot days while Negussie did laundry. In the rainy season, they trudged through the mud, not caring about the mess. They sprawled on the floor of the Coleman house, playing old board games, or inventing their own new games.

Negussie was at Murray and Bea's neat house so often that it almost seemed that he was one of their own children. Yet he proved to be a polite and helpful guest. God's good plans for Negussie included his ability, even at a young age, to teach and assist the Colemans.

At the kitchen table, he patiently taught the Oromo language. He also helped them improve their Amharic pronunciations because Negussie knew both languages. He graciously taught them about Ethiopian culture. This way, they could show kindness and respect to everyone around them. He would travel with Bea or Murray to meet their neighbors. He guided them on the best paths and helped them follow cultural courtesies. The Colemans loved Negussie and welcomed him gladly.

One day, in the middle of the long rainy season, Negussie looked outside the classroom window. The sky was relentless in its gray drizzle, and the yard was a gummy mess of mud. He knew the teacher would never let them play outside for recess. But then the teacher gave the class some

God's Child

excellent news. The Coleman family had invited all the children to their house! They would be playing games and learning stories from the Bible each day during this rainy week. Negussie was excited!

Bea welcomed the children at the door. They were careful not to bring in mud. Then, they sat with Murray. His blue eyes sparkled, and his Bible was open. It was during one of these lessons that Negussie understood that Jesus, the Son of God, came to forgive his sin and offer him eternal life. Negussie believed this teaching and prayed to ask Jesus to save him from his sins and become the Lord of his life. The dark clouds and rain outside were nothing like the bright new life in Negussie's heart. Now, he truly was God's child!

Murray and Bea were happy that Negussie joined God's family. They worked hard to teach him more about God and the Bible. God also brought other people to help Negussie in his young faith. One was a new nurse at Obi Station, named Chris Ott, who came from Germany. She taught Negussie's Sunday school class, and she noticed that Negussie longed to have a Bible for himself. But his family was poor and unlikely to buy him one. Bibles in local languages were rare and precious! Yet Negussie had learned how vitally important it was for a follower of Jesus to study and know the Bible.

Nurse Ott decided to make a contest in her Sunday school class. Anyone who memorized 200 Bible verses could win an Amharic Bible as a prize! Within only six weeks, Negussie had learned and recited every verse from memory and earned his very own Bible. Nurse Ott saw Negussie's strong commitment to God's word. So, she asked him to teach the Sunday school class for younger children.

Negussie loved reading the Bible!

Being at Obi Station also allowed Negussie to meet traveling pastors, preachers, and missionaries. They gathered there for conferences and meetings, offering him a chance to learn from them. One Ethiopian leader who visited was Pastor Kaydamo. Negussie listened closely as the tall man from the south spoke. He shared God's word with skill and humor. His heart was full of love for Jesus.

Negussie watched as Pastor Kaydamo talked. He noticed how the pastor would *listen* to the young men and give them wise counsel. God's kingdom needed faithful teachers and messengers from every part of Ethiopia. They would help build the church and bring people to Jesus. God was building a passion and desire in Negussie's heart to speak and share the good news with the people of Ethiopia.

At Obi Station and nearby churches, followers of Jesus would gather. Negussie noticed many Christians from different languages, regions, and backgrounds. They weren't split like much of Ethiopia, which is divided by Orthodox Christians and Islam, north and south, or various ethnic groups that often mistrust each other. The Christians were one family. And they all belonged to one king—not an Ethiopian emperor, but a heavenly King who loved them as his dear children.

Yet outside of this growing church of believers, Ethiopia remained divided along ethnic and religious lines. Many people hated the new Christians. This was true even though the Christians tried to live peacefully by offering hope and help through hospitals and schools.

It was not quite safe to declare that you were a part of this group of Christ followers. One of the most dangerous things was baptism. The Orthodox Church baptized babies following ancient traditions. This was quite different from the baptism taught at places like Obi Station and at Pastor Kaydamo's church.

Negussie was taught that those old enough to choose to follow Jesus should be baptized to declare their faith in God. Baptism was a demonstration to the community that a person belonged to Jesus in his death and resurrection. For those who held to the local religions, they worried that baptism would disrupt the spirits and bring them anger and punishment. To choose baptism was a step that could be quite costly for an Ethiopian believer—even causing some to be cut off from their family or rejected by friends.

Negussie studied his Bible and grew in faith. He learned from Bea, Murray, Pastor Kaydamo, Nurse Ott, and many other faithful teachers. He loved God, his heavenly Father. He knew that Jesus had died in his place to forgive him. He knew Jesus had brought him into God's family and would never reject him. The way was clear. Negussie would declare through baptism what his life was already showing—that he was God's child. A child of the King

He stepped into the river's current. Then, he went under the water as the pastor said, "In the name of the Father, the Son, and the Holy Spirit." He came up to the happy cheers of the people on the shore who watched this moment.

God's Child

This step of obedience to follow in Jesus's footsteps would set a pattern for the years ahead. Soon Negussie would face dangerous opposition to his faith. But Negussie would not back down or hide. Things were changing rapidly in Ethiopia. In the rocky green north, in the parched dry south, in the bustling city of Addis Ababa—trouble was brewing. The days ahead would not be easy.

Negussie's decision to be baptized took courage.

2

Revolution!

Negussie climbed aboard the already crowded bus. He smiled warmly at the passengers, but they returned only wary glances. Everyone seemed grim and unfriendly. The bus began rumbling down the road, jostling its passengers, and rocking the luggage that was precariously stacked on the roof above. It was a long trip. For three days, they twisted through narrow mountain passes. The bus jolted down rocky roads into steep valleys.

The year was 1974, and Negussie was headed north. He stared out the window of the bus as the rugged Ethiopian landscape changed before his eyes. So much had changed in his life as well. Negussie's childhood had ended. Many dear people had left the Obi missionary station and the nearby town of Wolisso. One friend had left to join the military. Another had gone away to the missionary Bible school. Others had left to become workers in medical clinics.

Negussie took a three-day bus journey to be trained as a teacher.

Pastor Kaydamo had moved into the capital city, Addis Ababa, to pastor a church there. And Negussie's dear family, the Colemans, had returned to Canada for one year. Missionaries often return home to visit the churches that support them with prayers and money. They share stories about what God is doing to encourage the believers who pray for them. The Colemans had another job on this trip to Canada. They were taking Negussie's best friend, John, back to finish high school in Alberta. That meant that when the Colemans returned to Ethiopia, John would not return with them.

There were days when Negussie felt forgotten and alone. He missed John, his faithful friend, most of all. Until one day, a thin, sealed letter arrived for him in the mail.

There was Negussie's name, scrawled in John's handwriting! John wrote to Negussie about what he missed in Ethiopia. He missed the spongey *injera* bread that soaked up spicy stews. He thought of the beautiful birds with their bright colors and unique shapes. The warm sunshine felt different sitting on a rock by a creek in Ethiopia compared to the Canadian prairies. He also missed the dear people and their familiar greetings and smiles.

John tried to help Negussie imagine his life in snowy, faraway Canada . . . his life in the dormitory at the high school, his schoolwork, his job at the dairy barn, and his efforts at learning to play the trumpet.

Negussie began to write John back, telling him about all the changes. He described his work teaching in the school at Obi, about the friends who had moved away, and about his efforts at learning to play the guitar. But the common thread in all the letters that flew back and forth between Canada and Ethiopia over those years was the messages of encouragement. The brothers promised one another that they would grow in faith and follow Jesus. They shared what God had been teaching them, and they wrote Bible verses to encourage their faraway friend.

As the bus bumped and bounced along another winding road, Negussie stared out the window and thought back through the letters he and John had sent. The letters were a great joy to Negussie, but he still felt as if the whole world had moved on from him.

When the Coleman family returned to Ethiopia without John, they moved away from Obi Station. First, they went to Addis Ababa, then to a leprosy clinic in Shashamane, south of Addis. Negussie began wondering what God's plans were for him now. In his letter to John that summer, he told him, "It is my decision to be a light for my Jesus anywhere, wherever it is." Negussie understood that no matter what happened, his mission stayed clear—to share the joy and hope of knowing Jesus with others.

Through writing these letters, Negussie began to realize he had been teaching others since he was a boy. From the time Nurse Ott asked him to teach Sunday school classes, or when he was sitting in Bea's kitchen reviewing her new Oromo words, he had been helping others understand. Perhaps God had created him to teach.

Negussie decided to apply to the Teacher Training Institute (TTI) to become a schoolteacher. TTI had training facilities throughout Ethiopia. However, a student could *not* choose which one they attended. Just a week before starting, Negussie learned he was accepted to a TTI school in Asmara, a city that was part of northern Ethiopia back then. This is why he was now on a bumpy three-day bus ride, far from the familiar life at Obi Station.

As the bus ventured further north, Negussie discovered things that shook him more than the hours on the rocky, winding roads. Outside the bus windows, there were frail, starving beggars on the roadside. They reached their spindly arms out, asking those passing by for something to eat. What was happening here? Why were there so many hungry people? And why hadn't Negussie heard anything about this?

You see, a lot had been happening in Ethiopia. First, there was a famine in the northern part of the country. There was not enough food, and people were starving to death. What's worse, the government tried to keep it a secret. They didn't want people to think they were doing a bad job running the country, so they hid the fact that thousands of people were dying from the food shortage. But despite their efforts to cover it up, lies and secrets cannot stay hidden. People were finding out and becoming increasingly angry with the leaders of Ethiopia.

Things were especially tense in the northern territory of Eritrea. Military groups rose to fight the Ethiopian government. They wanted Eritrea to separate and become its own country. In the north, soldiers were everywhere, and fighting could happen anywhere.

Throughout the whole country, the anger grew hotter and hotter. In the south, recruiters scooped up young men to fight in the war with Eritrea. Prices for everyday items were becoming prohibitively high. Poor people were being neglected and were the first to starve when famine hit.

Many people grew tired of the emperor and rich landowners. They saw them getting richer and gaining more power while common folks worked hard for little pay. People from all walks of life, like soldiers, taxi drivers, and university students, started to protest. They were against the government and the rich people. This led to major disruptions across the country. The streets swelled with people marching and chanting, refusing to work and yelling for change. Everyone was looking for answers to their problems—someone to blame or someone to change things.

All around the world, even today, there are many things that are unfair or wrong, and people are looking to find answers to their problems. Where should they turn? To God and his word! God has given us all we need to know in the Bible. He has shown us the way we should live, and how we can love and help one another. Jesus even told us that in this world we *will* have trouble (John 16:33), but we can be brave and hopeful. Why? Because we wait for the day when Jesus will return and make everything right. One day, the endless problems caused by sin will come to an end.

However, people often look to their own wisdom and the world's solutions to solve problems. And in Ethiopia, many people were not looking to God or the Bible for their answers. Instead, by the 1970s, many people were turning to an idea called "communism."

Communism was a theory spread by a man named Karl Marx over one hundred years earlier. Communists think no one should own land or factories. They believe this causes a few to get very rich while paying their workers very little.

Instead, they think the government should own everything—farms, mines, factories, and railroads. Then the government can take all the money and share it equally among all the people.

Communism started taking hold in Ethiopia.

It may seem like a nice idea at first. Sharing is a good thing, right? But unfortunately, the idea has a lot of flaws. In the end, it shifts power and wealth from rich business owners to the government. But the government is also made up of imperfect and greedy individuals. Communism has never worked, despite being tried many times worldwide.

Karl Marx also had specific ideas about how communism should happen. Here are two things you should know about this:

First, he believed that communism would begin with a *revolution*. This means that the poor and the working people would participate in a big rebellion. They would take everything away from the rich people and overthrow the government in power. If anyone fought against them, or disagreed with them, they could punish their opponents with prison, or beatings, or even death. A revolution would be disruptive and violent.

Does that sound like God's way? No! God says, "Let every person be subject to the governing authorities," and even that we are to "honor the emperor" (Romans 13:1; 1 Peter 2:17). God has given us a way to handle governments. We can give honor, speak truthfully, and rely on God, who is in charge of all power. But violence and rebellion are not God's way.

Second, Karl Marx believed that there should be no religion. No faith in God. He did not believe

God was real, and he thought that people who *did* believe in God were foolish. He thought that religious people would try to stop the revolution and work against communism. People who trusted in God to provide for their needs or help them in their struggle would not join a revolution. And so, Marx argued that following God should be banned under communism.

Negussie's old friend, Pastor Kaydamo, peeked through the blinds of the window in his church in Addis Ababa. He watched as another crowd of people moved down the busy street, with angry words scrawled across banners and pouring out of their mouths. He shook his head sadly. In the past months, he had seen people, even people in the church, enticed by the idea of communism. He was very concerned.

Pastor Kaydamo decided to spend a day in prayer and fasting, asking God to give him wisdom for the difficult days ahead. As he fervently pleaded with God for help, the Holy Spirit reminded him of Jesus's prayer in Gethsemane: "Not my will, but yours be done" (Luke 22:42). Jesus had been willing to obey the Father even to the point of death on a cross.

Pastor Kaydamo asked God to give him wisdom for the difficult days ahead.

In that moment, Pastor Kaydamo surrendered all his plans to God. If the churches were to be shut down, or the Bible banned, or if he and other pastors were to be thrown in jail or even killed, he thought, "Let it be, if it is God's will." Pastor Kaydamo was willing to die for his Lord Jesus. He breathed in deeply, feeling a great weight lift off his heart. In his commitment to Jesus, even if it meant death, he felt freedom to live through whatever was ahead of him.

In Ethiopia, a wave of rebellion swept through the people. Soon, a group of military leaders known as "The Derg" seized control of the country. They were led by a conniving and ambitious man known as Colonel Mengistu. The previous government leaders began to disappear. Some were arrested while others escaped to other countries.

Then, in September, on the Ethiopian New Year, the rebels captured the distinguished Ethiopian Emperor Haile Selassie. They shoved him down the steps of his palace into a small car waiting to take him away.

In November—the same month that Negussie traveled north for teacher training—things took an even darker turn. One morning, the Derg executed sixty of the former government officials they had arrested. Everything in Ethiopia had changed. Life had become uncertain and dangerous. Negussie and his classmates were soon evacuated from the Teacher Training Institute. They were moved to another town due to the violence with Eritrean fighters in Asmara.

As summer approached, Negussie was eager to travel back to Addis Ababa. It was a difficult and scary journey, but it was there that he had a joyful reunion with the Colemans. Even John, who had come to Ethiopia for his school break, was there!

John and Negussie's friendship remained strong through the years.

John and Negussie strolled through the streets of Addis, drinking sweet tea under the hot sun. They talked about how much life had changed.

And they rejoiced that their mutual love of Jesus remained steady as ever. Still, John couldn't help but worry about his friend. From Canada, he had watched the news coming out of Ethiopia. He had read in Negussie's careful letters that things were not stable. He knew that the missionary group that oversaw his parents was prepared for the day when the missionaries would be sent out of the country by the communists.

John glanced worriedly at Negussie, who continued to talk cheerfully, seemingly oblivious to the growing risk. John knew that Negussie socializing with a Westerner like him might be seen as "resisting the revolution." This could be risky for Negussie. Danger was ahead, and it was hard to think about leaving dear Negussie behind in Ethiopia to face it. When John did leave Ethiopia to return to Bible school in Canada, he sadly wondered when—or if—he would see his friend again.

By 1977, the communist leaders in Ethiopia became increasingly violent. They targeted anyone they thought *might* be an enemy. This time in

Ethiopia became known as the "Red Terror." People could be stopped at any time and commanded to show identification documents. Soldiers would not face any punishment if they decided to hurt the people they stopped. People were imprisoned, kidnapped, shipped across the country, or killed whenever a communist leader decided to do so.

In every city, village, and town throughout the country, there were people employed to spy on those around them and keep communist "order." They intimidated and punished anyone who went against the government or spoke about God.

Some young communists were sent to sit in church services in those days. As the pastor began to speak, they would yell and mock the Christians, calling them foolish for believing in God.

Sunday after Sunday, Negussie looked at the benches in the church as he strummed his guitar for the worship time. He noticed more and more empty seats each week. He worried about the people who had not come to church that day. Had they been harmed? Or had they decided to turn away from God?

People were missing from church as the revolution carried on.

Negussie wrote to John about friends who had once claimed to follow Jesus but had now left him behind. People were facing pressure to leave the church and reject Jesus. Negussie said that every Christ follower had to decide whether "to stay or go." But for Negussie, he would never leave Christ. He wrote to John, "In Jesus, I find full comfort and blessings. I am confident in my decision to follow God."

At one church service, a communist squad declared that religion had no place in the new

Ethiopia. They scorned the people for praying. A peasant woman stood up among those gathered. "In spite of all you have told us," she said in a calm and firm voice, "we came here to pray to God, and we're going to pray before we leave." They immediately charged her with resisting the revolution and roughly hurried her down to the police station.

When she was finally released from her arrest, they warned and threatened her to stop her ridiculous religious ways. She promptly invited her communist accusers to come to her house for a home-cooked meal. As she served them the freshly made *injera* flatbread and aromatic meat stew, she invited them to pray with her for the meal. Instead, they laughed loudly and tried to drown out her steady voice as she prayed confidently to God, her Defender and Provider.

By 1978, most people from other countries had fled Ethiopia, including many missionaries. But Murray and Bea Coleman were determined to stay as long as they could, even if it was dangerous.

Revolution!

They watched as their Ethiopian brothers and sisters in the church were mocked, persecuted, and thrown into jail. The Colemans knew that their fair complexions and "Western ways" made them targets as enemies of the communist revolution. They had to be careful with every step.

It was a scary and discouraging time for Christians. The small group of missionaries that remained amid the violence and hatred searched for ways to encourage the Ethiopian believers.

In England during this time, a pastor named Yu Kwong Hsueh and his wife, Lily, visited a college. There, some African students shared what was happening in Ethiopia. Pastor Hsueh had worked in churches and missions in Malaysia, the Philippines, and China. He had experience with communism. He had lived through the communist revolution in China during the 1940s and '50s. He had fled danger and knew Chinese Christians who had been imprisoned or killed for following Jesus.

Because he was from Asia, Pastor Hsueh was free to travel around Ethiopia.

Murray Coleman had a friend, Paul Balisky, who ran the nearby Bible college. They invited Pastor Hsueh to come teach the Ethiopian church about his experiences living through persecution. Murray and Paul had to be extremely careful about what they did. As white Westerners, they were seen as enemies by the communists.

However, Murray and Paul quickly noticed that Pastor Hsueh was treated very differently. Because he was Asian, the communist soldiers and officials assumed he was an important Chinese communist. They allowed him to travel through checkpoints with ease and respect! They would whisper, "This Chinaman must be from the Derg! Let him through!"

And so, Pastor Hsueh was free to travel around Ethiopia. He held secret meetings with Bible college students, churches, and Christians who had been put in prison for their faith in God. Murray and Paul chuckled at the way God provided safe passage for Pastor Hsueh through communist territory to spread hope in Jesus.

Pastor Hsueh shared how God stayed faithful to Chinese Christians during tough times. He assured the Ethiopian believers that because God had been faithful before, he would be again in this revolution. He encouraged the Ethiopians to face persecution with bravery that came from trusting in God. He turned the beloved pages of his Bible to John 19. From that passage, he reminded them that Jesus's friend John was the only disciple to stay with Jesus through his crucifixion. Everyone else ran away in fear and shame. He challenged the Ethiopians to be like the disciple John. By God's grace they could continue in faith with courage. He longed for them to stay with Jesus to the end.

People started meeting secretly in homes.

More and more, church meetings and Bible studies had to meet in secret. Negussie was traveling through Addis Ababa one week in 1978. While there, he joined a secret church group in the home of a believer, as he often would. His heart was refreshed as the believers sang confidently together about their good God. Together they bowed their heads over the Bible passage, filling their hungry hearts with truth. They prayed urgently to God to provide a way through these dark and scary days of the revolution, and to help their many friends in need.

While Negussie's heart felt full from the fellowship of gathering with believers, his heart felt delight in something else as well. Across the room was a young woman he had not met before. She was beautiful. She had warm bronze skin and thick wavy hair. She carried herself with strength and elegance, but her smile was gentle, and her eyes crinkled with kindness.

Negussie made his way back to Wolisso that evening, where he now worked as a schoolteacher. As he waded through the lengthening shadows cast by the setting sun, he should have been thinking about his lessons for school the next day. But his mind and heart kept racing back to that young woman. Would their paths ever cross again? Would she ever think twice about him? He was only a poor country teacher, with his body stunted

God's Child

and hunched from his childhood tuberculosis. He didn't know. But as he made the journey home, he prayed to his God who knows all things.

3

Love and Terror

You are most fortunate! Because, while poor Negussie was wondering and waiting to find out more about the young woman at the church gathering, you can read ahead to find out more.

Her name was Fantaye. She was from the city of Addis Ababa. She was well educated, and her family was wealthy, Amhara, and Orthodox. She grew up following the traditions and rules of the Orthodox church. But while she found the church festivals and traditions beautiful and familiar, she still felt empty inside. It didn't seem that the Orthodox church had answers to her questions about life. She was searching for something more.

A friend of Fantaye's suggested she look for answers in the Bible. She could also listen to Bible teachings on the Addis radio station, RVOG, which means "Radio Voice of the Gospel."

Fantaye listens to Bible teaching on the radio.

Fantaye heard crackles and buzzing as she turned the radio dial to find the station her friend had suggested. A voice speaking Amharic carried over the airwaves of her radio and trickled into her room. At the same time, God's truth poured into her heart.

She heard that her sin had separated her from God. That is why she felt so empty inside! And no number of traditions or rituals or good deeds could ever make her right with God. No, there was a price for her sin, and that price had to be paid. That price was death.

The name "Fantaye" sounds like the Amharic words for "instead of me." Fantaye learned that, while *she* deserved to be punished for her sins, *Jesus* had paid the price *instead of her*. God loved her, and he gave his only Son, Jesus Christ, to come and take her place. Jesus paid the penalty for her sin by dying on the cross instead of her. Because Jesus is God, his payment was enough, and he rose from the grave on the third day. He now reigns in heaven and will return one day to bring all who have trusted in him to enjoy eternal life with him.

Fantaye listened as the faraway voice explained that she must believe in Jesus, trusting in him to wash her sins away. She learned that Jesus could give her new life—spiritual life—to fill her and change her to be more like him.

Fantaye believed. Jesus and his gift of forgiveness were what she had been needing and wanting more than anything else in the world. She began regularly listening to the radio broadcast and studying the Bible to know more.

But one day, the communist officers stormed into the RVOG radio station and shut everything down. They would no longer allow the Bible to be broadcast to the people of Ethiopia. They despised and feared the message of the Bible. It gave people hope and purpose apart from their violent revolution, and it had to be silenced.

Instead, they would broadcast propaganda. This meant that the radio announcers would spew lies about the "glory" of the communist revolution and the "successes" of Ethiopia under the new Derg government. This propaganda tried to justify the violent punishment of anyone who would speak or act against communism.

Without the radio programs to continue teaching her, Fantaye began to seek out the secret churches. They met quietly in homes around the city. There, she could learn more from the Bible. She could worship with others who had trusted in Jesus and be encouraged to continue in the faith she'd found. It was at one of these underground church gatherings that Negussie and Fantaye's paths crossed.

Negussie spent the next day at school distractedly thinking back to Fantaye. But Fantaye had not thought much about this new fellow visiting from Wolisso. At first, he had stood out to her because he was different. He was short, with stooped shoulders and a mature face. She wondered what had made him that way. But when she saw his radiant smile, she felt at ease in his presence.

It wasn't until his next trip through Addis that she thought more about him. For their church gathering, he played his guitar as the group sang. She watched as he strummed the chords and sang from his heart to Jesus, whom he so clearly loved.

Only a month before they met for the first time, Fantaye had prayed, asking God to provide her with a godly husband. She longed to marry a man who truly loved Jesus. In her family and at work, she felt so different and alone since she had given her life to Jesus. She hoped for a husband to follow Jesus alongside her.

This was not what Fantaye's family hoped for her, however. They participated in the Orthodox patterns of life while trying to avoid any trouble from the communist government. They had ensured that Fantaye had received a good education, and they were proud of her for getting a good job as an accountant in the Ministry of Health. Fantaye knew her family wanted her to marry an Orthodox man with a well-to-do family like hers.

After that second church gathering was over, Negussie worked up the courage to approach Fantaye. She welcomed him with kindness. He asked her if it would be alright for the two to keep in touch by sending letters. Fantaye said "yes," and watched as that shining smile spread across Negussie's face in relief and joy.

While Negussie nearly floated back to Wolisso that day, Fantaye thought about Negussie. Why was she so drawn to him? He was not wealthy, or influential, or sophisticated, or even particularly handsome by the world's standards. But Fantaye could see in him what mattered most—he loved Jesus more than anything. His faith in Jesus made him more rich, powerful, wise, and beautiful than the world could ever make him.

In the weeks and months to come, Negussie could barely contain himself from running to the post office in Wolisso. Letters from John, and now letters from Fantaye, could brighten even the cloudiest day.

The situation in Ethiopia continued to worsen.

Yet the days in Ethiopia were indeed getting darker. In region after region, missionaries were being sent away. Church leaders were being harassed and arrested, and people were leaving behind the way of Jesus for communism. And in every place, it was hard to know who to trust.

News came that the government shut down the Bible college. Angry protestors expelled the missionaries. Paul Balisky, the school's director who had arranged for Pastor Hsueh's visits, was accused of being a spy and forced to leave.

One day, Negussie received a letter about an old friend. He had been killed in a battle in the war for Eritrean independence. People Negussie and Fantaye had known would mysteriously disappear without a trace. In some places, churches were burned down to only heaps of wreckage and ashes.

Fantaye would walk the streets of Addis on her way to work and see people lying on the roadside. They had been killed by communist soldiers. Often, a note was pinned to them. The note accused them of crimes against the revolution that led to their brutal death.

At Fantaye's office, people were increasingly suspicious. They wondered who was loyal to the government, and who might get reported to the authorities because of jealousy or rumors. Fantaye was shrewd to avoid attention as she snuck away to her secret church meetings, hiding her Bible in the folds of her clothing. All around her there was fear and anger and suffering.

Meanwhile, the city was draped in bold red banners, flaunting large pictures of communist leaders. Parades loudly twisted through the streets and squares declaring that communism was victorious.

In Wolisso, Negussie and the other teachers had to attend weekly meetings with officials from the government. The classes aimed to teach them about communism. The officials also tried to intimidate the teachers into sharing this message with their students.

Negussie sat quietly in the meetings, enduring the harsh speeches and pressure from the leaders. These "training" meetings were intended to convince him that communism was "the way," but it had the opposite effect on him. He knew that Jesus was the only way, the truth, and the life (John 14:6). He knew that Jesus did not need to bluster and shout to convince him. It was Jesus's kindness and love that had drawn Negussie's heart to believe. He knew that Jesus did not need violence or cruelty to get his way or show his power. Jesus was the all-powerful God, and yet he had stooped down to wash the disciples' feet. His hands were nailed to a cross. Negussie would never change his mind about Jesus, no matter how hard the communists tried.

Negussie showed his students the love of Jesus.

First John 4:4 says, "Little children, you are from God and have overcome them, for he who is in you is greater than he who is in the world."

Negussie was God's child. He knew that God was greater than any boastful government could ever be. And he had God's Holy Spirit to help him through whatever he would face. Negussie could have hope knowing that he would overcome this time of terror with God's care.

Negussie decided that he would follow the government's rules as far as he could. He would be respectful and polite, but he would not sin against God in the process. If a government rule opposed God, he would not cooperate.

This meant that Negussie would not stop sharing the gospel of Jesus with those around him, even though it was forbidden. Jesus had commanded believers to go and make disciples, so that is what Negussie did. He welcomed his students into his classroom and showed them the love of Jesus. As he got to know them better, they would ask questions about his hope and joy.

Negussie began a Bible study for all the students who were interested. He was able to get small New Testament Bibles, which he shared with any student who asked. He had to be careful about what he said in the classroom. But in the evenings, students stopped by his home to ask him questions about spiritual things.

The communist leaders in Wolisso began keeping a close eye on Negussie. They saw the way the students were drawn to this kind, humble, hopeful man, and they wanted to get rid of him.

Without warning, Negussie received a notice. He was being relocated to another school in a place called Gindo. This didn't make any sense. He had been promoted several times at Wolisso, and he was known as an effective and popular teacher. But now he was being sent to a small, poor school, deep in the countryside. This was a humiliating step down for a teacher of his experience. And he knew no one in the isolated community he was being sent to. Negussie let Fantaye know that he would be moving further away and that he would have even less opportunity to see her.

But as Negussie had promised John years before in a letter, he was determined to be a light for Jesus anywhere, wherever it is. So, he continued to teach and love his students and share with them about his hope in Jesus in the community of Gindo. Yet, in this new school, the communists continued to watch Negussie. They noted who visited his house or stayed after school, and they kept track of his comings and goings.

On a day off, Negussie was finally able to make a trip to Addis to see Fantaye. She brought him some Bible tracts. They were neat little pamphlets with Bible verses and explanations about God's good news. Negussie was so grateful for such a gift! In the small rural village, people didn't have many books. These would be eagerly received. But even more, they would clearly show people the way of salvation in Jesus.

Negussie's broad, bright grin met Fantaye's shy smile. Though their time together was brief, it showed that their faith in Jesus united them. Even living far apart, their hearts were moving in the same direction.

Fantaye sneaked away to attend a secret Bible study.

Soon after handing the gift to Negussie, Fantaye said goodbye and walked briskly and quietly to a church meeting. Her Bible was tucked securely inside her sweater, and her eyes darted through the shadowy streets for any signs of trouble. She entered the meeting and greeted her fellow Jesus-followers, who had each made a similar careful journey there that night.

They prayed together urgently and studied the Bible eagerly. But somehow, someone must have given away the location and purpose of their secret meeting that night. Soldiers came crashing into the room. They arrested Fantaye and the other believers and herded them to jail.

By this time in the revolution, the communists had arrested and captured so many people as "enemies of communism" that the jails were full. So, they had taken over other buildings and turned them into haphazard prisons. Fantaye and her brothers and sisters in Christ were kept locked away day after day, without a hearing or fair trial to accuse them of any specific crime. But, because there was no space to keep them, they were released after a few weeks.

As soon as Fantaye was set free, she made her way to the post office. She expected a letter from Negussie waiting for her! He would be wondering why she hadn't replied to this letter yet. As she hurried to the post office, she anticipated the heartfelt message in his elegant handwriting. But when she arrived, she was confused. There was no letter. No letter? This was not like faithful, friendly Negussie. He had been in Gindo for six months now, and the lonely, boring little town had only meant his letters had become *more* frequent. Her heart dropped.

She wanted to let Negussie know what had happened to her over the last few weeks. She quickly wrote to him about her arrest and time in jail, but she also assured him that she was free and healthy. She composed the message in coded language that only Negussie would be able to understand, in case her letter was opened and read by the authorities. She was sure once Negussie heard what had happened, he would respond.

Days went by, and Fantaye waited for his letter to come. Still, it didn't. This was so unlike Negussie! Surely, he would care deeply about what had happened to her!

Finally, she decided to take a risk by calling him on the phone to ask what had happened. A voice on the other line answered gruffly. She asked to speak with Negussie Kumbi. The response was short. "Negussie is not here."

Fantaye felt like all the blood in her body had turned to ice as she processed this fearful news. Not there? Where was he? All these weeks without a letter? What had happened to dear Negussie?

4

Ready to Die and Free to Live

Once again, we leave our character—this time, Fantaye—waiting and wondering.

Remember, Fantaye had brought Negussie a gift the last time they had seen each other. It was a bundle of little tracts—booklets that had Bible verses and explained the way to be saved through Jesus. Negussie had also managed to get some more of the small New Testaments that he used to give away in Wolisso.

Negussie hurried back to Gindo, holding these treasured books close to his chest. His heart was flying from seeing Fantaye in person. But even more, he was encouraged by how well she knew him to bring him these precious tracts. As he traveled, he thought through each of his students, and he prayed that they might receive the tracts with gladness.

It wasn't long after returning to Gindo that a few students visited him at his home. He invited them in for tea and welcomed their questions. Negussie joyfully shared with them his story of how he had come to be God's child. He explained how they could trust in God as their Father too. Before they left, he gave each one a tract and a small New Testament to take home.

Soon after, some of Negussie's fellow teachers visited him. They had heard that the students had received New Testaments from Negussie, and they asked if they could each have one as well. As kind as ever, Negussie gladly gave them a copy of God's word.

But by the end of the week, everything turned against Negussie. Classes for the day were canceled so that the whole community could attend a rally to celebrate communism. As Negussie sat through the rambling speeches, suddenly the two teachers who had visited him at night rose up out of the crowd. They pointed at Negussie, and the eyes of the crowd followed their fingers to land on the small, humble man.

The teachers loudly declared that Negussie was a traitor to the revolution. They had proof that he had been acting against the government by spreading a "foreign" religion and handing out anti-communist literature. They held up the slim New Testaments as proof. Negussie's heart fell. The same book he had worked hard to earn as a child by memorizing verses was now used against him.

Officials and soldiers stomped through the crowd to take Negussie to jail. All his belongings were searched. In Negussie's few possessions, they found letters from John Coleman and Fantaye. They clutched the letters tightly in their fists. This was proof of Negussie's betrayal of communist Ethiopia. They rushed him to the police station in Wolisso.

In many communist countries, and certainly in Ethiopia at that time, anything from the Western world—Canada, Europe, and especially the United States—was seen as the enemy. Negussie's accusers saw the letters from John, which were written in English and had foreign postmarks. They concluded that these must be letters from a *spy* in the CIA. (CIA stands for Central Intelligence Agency, the organization in the United States for American spy and surveillance work.) This was an unlikely conclusion. John was just a humble young Bible college student in Three Hills, Alberta, Canada. But the details were ignored, and the claim that Negussie was a CIA spy stuck.

To heap more shame upon Negussie, they presented his letters from Fantaye as evidence that he was having an inappropriate relationship with a woman. This was, of course, absurd. Negussie had been careful to obey God's ways. He had treated Fantaye with utmost respect and dignity as his sister in Christ. But the contents of the letters were overlooked, and the allegations against Negussie were assumed.

To add to the charges, an older Orthodox priest claimed that Negussie was a religious fanatic. He said that Negussie was spreading a foreign religion that didn't belong in proud Ethiopia.

How do you think Negussie felt as these angry men heaped all these accusations on him?

How would you feel if people lied about you and said you were doing horrible things that you were not doing? In that moment, Negussie's experience was just like his Lord Jesus'. Jesus had also been arrested unfairly. People told lies about Jesus and accused him of horrible, untrue things. Negussie had peace knowing that Jesus knew exactly how he felt because Jesus had been through it too.

The soldiers arrested Negussie!

That very night, they hurried Negussie away to Wolisso. As they stumbled through the darkness, Negussie remembered that he had a small flashlight with him. In his typical kindness, Negussie offered to light their way to make the journey easier. To the old Orthodox priest, he showed respect. He carefully helped him on the difficult journey over rocks, branches, and brambles. Even on that dark night, as Negussie stumbled toward certain danger, he shone the light of Jesus, just as he shone the light from his little flashlight.

At Wolisso, the mob laid out their case against him. Negussie politely but firmly told them the truth. He was most certainly *not* a political spy working for a foreign country. But he admitted that he *was* a member of God's kingdom. He would not deny that he was God's child. The officers baited him with an offer. "If you simply reject this foreign religion, we'll let you go free."

Negussie responded, "I would rather die than deny my Lord."

It was just like Pastor Kaydamo had concluded at the start of the revolution. Being willing to *die* for Jesus gave the believers incredible confidence to *live* for Jesus. Negussie was like Shadrach, Meshach, and Abednego facing the fiery furnace. He knew his God could save him from anything. But even if God chose not to save him, Negussie would not back down from his faith in God. Negussie did not have to fear death because he was confident that through Jesus's gift of forgiveness, he would have eternal life in heaven.

The accusers scoffed at Negussie. "Your choice." They shook their heads at this foolish man who wouldn't simply deny his religion and go free. By this time in Ethiopia, there were few rules or restraints for police and communist leaders. In many cases, they tortured their prisoners. They tried to harm them so badly that the prisoner would admit to crimes or turn from the things they were doing.

For poor Negussie, they tied him up and covered his mouth with a gag. They hung him between two tables and beat the bottoms of his feet with a heavy stick. Negussie's feet became covered with blisters and blood. They looked terrible.

But do you know what God says? In Romans 10:15 the Bible tells us, "How beautiful are the feet of those who preach the good news!" It was because Negussie had faithfully preached the good news of Jesus that his feet were being beaten, and God saw them as beautiful.

After a long time, the officer ripped the gag from Negussie's mouth. "Are you ready to reject your religion?" he shouted. Negussie gasped for air and spoke without wavering, "I am ready to die for my Lord Jesus Christ!"

Enraged, the officers beat Negussie's entire body with renewed cruelty. The only thing that finally stopped their attack was laziness. They decided they did not want to deal with a dead body that night, and so they stopped before Negussie could die.

Negussie had once again walked on the same path as Jesus. Jesus had also been beaten and bloodied by cruel accusers. Jesus knew his pain.

The guards heaved Negussie's broken body onto the floor of the prison cell. As he lay in a heap, he was sure that he was dying, or even dead. But as he thought about his Father God, he felt life stirring in him. He was certain in that moment that God wanted him to live. His story was not over.

It would be weeks before Negussie could walk again. He had to depend on the criminals in the prison to carry him, even to go to the bathroom. His body was unrecognizable from the gashes and bruises and swelling. The only clues to his identity were his hunched back and his bright smile. No matter how much he suffered, that smile never faded.

Finally, he managed to send a note out of the prison with someone traveling to Addis Ababa. He had to tell Fantaye where he was.

As Fantaye unfolded the crumpled slip of paper, she saw Negussie's familiar handwriting. Her heart flooded with relief and joy. Negussie was alive! But the relief evaporated quickly when she read the message. Negussie was in the Wolisso jail.

Fantaye briefly visited Negussie in prison.

As soon as she could, Fantaye made the trip to Wolisso. She wrapped some fresh fruit in a handkerchief to give to Negussie. She remembered her terrible hunger during her own time in jail. When she arrived, however, the guards would not let her in.

"Please!" she wept. "My dear brother, Negussie Kumbi is here! I must see him!" Of course, she knew the guards did not really understand what she meant by "brother." But in her heart, she knew it was true! She was God's child. Negussie was God's child. In their heavenly Father's family, they were brother and sister. Finally, the guards allowed her in, but only for five short minutes.

As Negussie saw Fantaye coming toward him, his vision blurred with hot tears. Those tears washed down his dirt-stained cheeks as his heart swelled with joy. But Fantaye's heart broke at the sight of dear Negussie. His appearance was more stooped and broken than ever before.

Fantaye felt helpless. How she wanted to get him free from that jail and get him the medical help he clearly needed. But she could not help him. As she was roughly escorted out of their brief meeting, she prayed to her Father in heaven. He was the only one who could help Negussie.

That summer, John came back to Ethiopia to take a break from Bible college. On the long flight over the Atlantic Ocean, John longed to feel the hot African sunshine on his face. He wanted to smell the dark Ethiopian coffee. But more so, he was eager to see his family. He knew his parents,

Murray and Bea, had been through so much in the days of the Red Terror. He had eagerly read their carefully worded letters. He had scoured the Canadian newspapers for any snippets of information about what was happening in communist Ethiopia. And he was eager to see the friend who was a brother to him, Negussie Kumbi.

Soon after the plane landed, John heard the news about Negussie. John wanted so badly to go and see his dear friend at the jail, but he knew that his presence there would do more harm than good. If a white Westerner were to visit Negussie at the prison, that would only strengthen the accusers' claims that he was a traitor to the Ethiopian revolution. John's company would surely condemn Negussie.

Instead, the Colemans decided to send a gift with the most practical purpose possible. They prepared a package with a special bug-repellent soap. This would help Negussie with the fleas and bugs that infested the prison.

Negussie sent a gift to the Colemans with a secret message.

Before long, John received a precious gift in return. A pastor named Tekle had visited Negussie at the prison. Through the rusted bars, Negussie entrusted Tekle with a package for the Colemans. There was also some money that Negussie had managed to earn selling woven crafts in the jail. It was his tithe for the church. He wanted it to be used to help and encourage the believers.

Murray, Bea, and John gathered around the package delivered to them from Pastor Tekle, who had told them of Negussie's joy and generosity, even in the middle of his suffering. Out of the package, they carefully lifted a hat that Negussie had woven. Inside the hat were instructions for how to wash and stretch it for wearing. Then, John noticed something else inside the hat. Behind the washing instructions was a note carefully tucked away. Bea's eyes sparkled with delight as she saw it was, in fact, a secret message for them:

> To my dear friend John and all my family:
>
> Daily God gives me unspeakable joy and comfort. I am completely well and healthy. I have received the soap you sent me.
> May God bless you. If God wills, I hope to see you after I receive the verdict. Acts 20:24, Phil 1:20.
>
> I am sending this small gift to my brother, John.
>
> I am your son,
>
> Negussie Kumbi

Murray reached for his well-worn Bible, and his fingers traced the pages to find the verses that Negussie referred to:

> *However, I consider my life worth nothing to me; my only aim is to finish the race and complete the task the Lord Jesus has given me—the task of testifying to the good news of God's grace.* (Acts 20:24 NIV)
>
> *I eagerly expect and hope that I will in no way be ashamed, but will have sufficient courage so that now as always Christ will be exalted in my body, whether by life or by death.* (Philippians 1:20 NIV)

Murray's face, now more creased from the hard years of the revolution, crinkled into a smile. That was Negussie. Faithful as always.

Negussie had hoped the results of his court case would bring him freedom and the ability to see his loved ones, but it did not. Rather, Fantaye learned that he would be moved to Addis Ababa, but remain a prisoner. It pained her to go about her daily life. Working, eating, sleeping in her comfortable bed . . . seeing friends and family each day . . . it all felt out of place when she knew that Negussie was nearby, but in a cramped cell with rats to torment him at night.

Eventually, Fantaye heard an update. Negussie was being transferred to the large prison in Addis. Hope mingled with despair. At the overcrowded prison she might be able to slip in unnoticed to see him! But this prison had an infamous nickname—*Alem Beckagn*—which means "the end of the world." Many prisoners who went there never came out. An ominous question flickered in Fantaye's heart: Would this be the end for Negussie?

Fantaye was determined to go see him. Once again, she wrapped some fruit in a small pouch and made her way to the prison. She stepped into the lineup of women who had come to bring gifts or greetings to their imprisoned husbands. As she found herself at the front of the line, she stepped forward and raised her package of fruit so that

Negussie might see her. He ran toward her, and they met at the fence as she handed him her gift. He had nothing to offer her in return but his broad smile. She looked into his eyes, and that was enough.

Over the next months, Fantaye came week after week, hoping they could look each other in the eye and exchange a few brief words through the prison fence. But her heart ached. She wished that Negussie could be free, and they could really, truly *begin* their life together. Instead, all they had were a few fleeting moments at "the *end* of the world."

Negussie, however, continued in the promise he had made to be a light for Jesus "anywhere, wherever it is." God had brought him to this prison, so this was where God had work for him to do. Even those who staunchly refused Negussie's gospel invitations could not deny that Negussie lived each day with hope and joy. He patiently counseled, encouraged, and prayed with anyone who would receive his friendship.

Soon he found a few other believers in the prison. They began a secret church and called it,

"The Invisible Fellowship Church." At one point, they managed to get a Bible into the prison. They carefully separated the binding of the book and divided the contents into sections—each with some pages of scripture.

Negussie's secret church in prison divided a Bible and shared the sections.

By that time, there were over 70 people in the prison who had trusted in Jesus as their Savior. They each received their little slice of the Bible and studied it for a week. Then, on Thursdays, they discreetly traded for another piece of the Bible as they passed each other in the bathroom.

They all worked carefully to keep their church "invisible" from the guards. Soon, the 70 Christians turned into 300 among the prisoners. They all wanted to learn about the bold hope the believers had in such a hopeless place. How much harder it was to remain "invisible" when there were so many of them!

Finally, one day, Negussie and several of the other organizers of the Invisible Fellowship Church were removed from their cells and taken far away from the other prisoners. As they were shoved down the dark hallways, they glanced with wide, knowing eyes at one another. They were headed toward the rooms known as the "death cells." Surely, the guards had found out that they had organized a church in the prison. They were certain that they were indeed facing the end.

Day after day, for 15 days, they waited in the "death cells." But as they waited, they enjoyed a peculiar freedom. The guards already knew that they had brought the message of the Bible into the jail. So why hide it now? In those days, as they waited to be killed, they prayed together openly and sang songs of worship freely. They no longer needed to be invisible. Even if their lives were taken from them, their hope in God could never be taken away.

Then, after 15 days, Negussie was notified. It was time for his meeting with the prison warden.

5

The Finish Line

I know you are nearly as eager as Negussie to find out his fate in the warden's office. But first, we must go back and understand what else had been happening while Negussie was in prison. Remember that Fantaye would visit Negussie each week at the prison. Six years went by while he was locked inside, and Fantaye waited for him.

    Fantaye's family could not understand her. She was a smart, beautiful young woman with a good job. Why did she waste her time reading the Bible or sneaking off to the underground church services? And why was she so committed to that odd man in the prison? The one who was poor and deformed and came from the countryside? As was the tradition, young men visited Fantaye's family, each one hoping to arrange for her to become his bride. But each time an eager suitor visited, Fantaye politely declined the offer.

Fantaye and Negussie had already promised each other that they would marry. Fantaye remembered the prayer she had prayed just one week before meeting Negussie for the first time. She had asked the Lord for a husband who loved Jesus. She had prayed to her heavenly Father, "I want only the one you want for me."

Negussie had told Fantaye, "I have no wealth and not much knowledge, but I have Jesus Christ in my heart, so I have everything. This is all I can offer you." And so, the two had prayerfully believed that it was God's plan for them to be married one day.

But as the years of Negussie's imprisonment dragged on, both Fantaye and Negussie wondered if they were doing the right thing. Negussie had heard in the prison that his good friend John had married his love—a smart, spirited blonde woman named Phyllis. He was happy for John, but it deepened his guilt that Fantaye seemed to be wasting her time anticipating Negussie's freedom.

Fantaye was old enough that she could be getting married, setting up a home, and raising children. But instead, each week she made the difficult and lonely bus trip to visit Negussie and speak only a few words before she was shuffled out. Negussie had told Fantaye that if she wanted to be free of her promise to him, that was OK. But she responded that she would not let him go.

Now, Negussie took slow, echoing steps down the long, grimy corridor. He had been called out from the death cell to the prison warden's office, along with the other prisoners who had organized the Invisible Fellowship Church. This group of men had shared one Bible among many prisoners. They had prayed, counseled, and taught the message of salvation to anyone who would listen.

Negussie was certain that he was facing death, but he had peace. Jesus had died for him. He would die for Jesus. And in the end, he would be *with* Jesus.

The warden began by yelling at them, shaming their antirevolutionary acts. But then, as he spoke, something inside him changed. He began apologizing for the cruel treatment of the men. He confessed that they did not deserve it. He saw the believers were different from other prisoners. They lived with dignity, hope, and peace. By the end of the meeting in his office, the shocked men were told that they were free to leave the prison. They had completed their sentence.

On a spring day in 1986, as the breezes lilted with a hopeful scent of new beginnings in the air, Fantaye received a note:

She should come. There was a celebration. Negussie was free!

Negussie was finally free!

Fantaye walked timidly into a crowded house in Addis Ababa. The room was filled with Negussie's friends and relatives rejoicing over his freedom, each waiting for their turn to greet him. When it was finally her turn to approach him, he hugged her tightly. There was no longer a prison fence between them. Tears of joy streamed down Fantaye's face.

Negussie told the story over and over to the astonished group. The warden had gruffly summoned him to his office, but what followed was simply a miracle. And God had rescued Negussie from jail.

Murray, Bea, and John received the news in Canada with great gladness. It had pained Murray and Bea to leave the believers in Ethiopia. To watch them suffer from a distance broke their hearts. As soon as news of Negussie's release came, Bea sat down at her typewriter and wrote out as many details of Negussie's story as she could recall. She wanted to be sure people would remember his story.

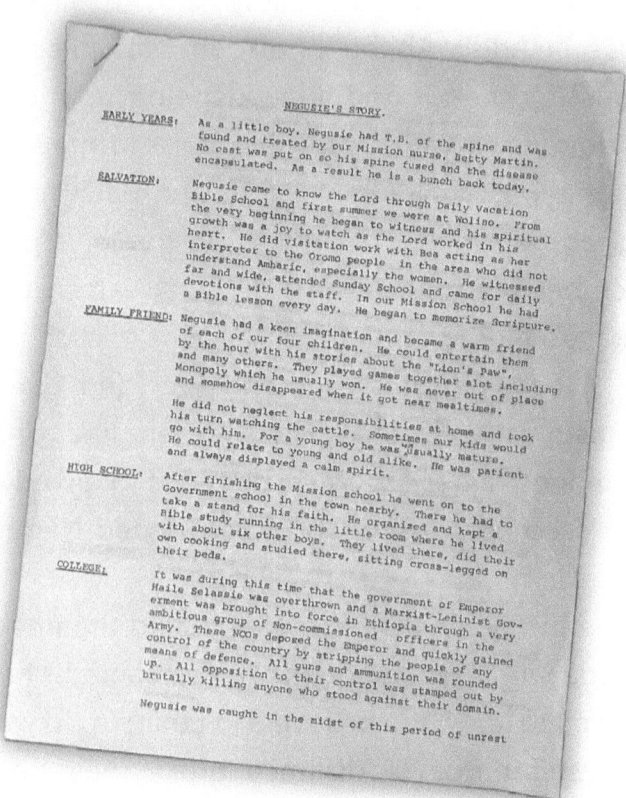

Bea began writing about Negussie's life.

But just because he was free, it did not mean things were easy. There was no way Negussie could return to a teaching position now, with the government controlling the schools. And as a former prisoner, it made it difficult for him to find any job at all. He did not have the money he needed to pay for a home and get married to Fantaye. Besides that, Fantaye's family had not approved their plans to marry. Negussie and Fantaye would have to wait a little longer.

Negussie went from job to job, working wherever and however he could. But no steady work came. The country had grown poorer, and famine had ravaged many regions. Negussie wondered once again about God's plans for his life. As he waited, he faithfully attended his old friend Pastor Kaydamo's church in Addis Ababa.

You see, a very mysterious thing happened. Most church buildings had been condemned and nailed shut by this point in the revolution. But Pastor Kaydamo's church, located in a busy part of the city, remained untouched. The congregation continually prayed for their freedom and protection, and it seemed that God had set a shield around them.

As life became more and more miserable in Ethiopia, more and more people began coming through the doors of the church, seeking truth and hope. The congregation was overflowing. They added more service times and held programs and classes throughout the week. Negussie served the church faithfully in any way he could.

Negussie served faithfully at church.

One day, Pastor Kaydamo asked to speak with him. He and some other leaders in the Ethiopian church had seen Negussie's heart for Jesus and God's word. They saw Negussie's many gifts and abilities. They wanted to offer Negussie a scholarship to go to seminary at Scott College in

Kenya. This was a special high-level school to train ministry workers. This was the answer Negussie had been waiting for! The Lord had laid a path before him to serve the church of Ethiopia, just as Negussie had hoped to do from his youth. Getting his travel documents to leave Ethiopia for Kenya was dreadfully hard under the government regime. But, in a miracle that assured him of God's care, he quickly received all the approval he needed.

Fantaye joined Negussie in Kenya.

In Kenya, Negussie joyfully immersed himself in learning and study at the Bible college. But it had been 12 long years since his eyes had first met

Fantaye's in that secret church meeting in Addis. As he read her letters, he tried to imagine her speaking to him in her gentle, warm voice. He decided he needed to try once more to ask her family for permission to marry. He sent some of his relatives and community leaders to go to her family's house in Addis Ababa and seek their approval. This time, they gave their permission!

Before long, Fantaye's family saw her off on a flight to Nairobi, Kenya, where she would join her groom, Negussie.

Many of their family and friends were unable to make the trip to Kenya for the wedding. But as he did everywhere else, Negussie had been serving faithfully at the local church. Many people there had fallen in love with this cheerful, resilient man. For their wedding, the whole church came together—rich and poor, young and old, Ethiopian and Kenyan—providing food for the reception, film for the photos, and cars for the procession. In fact, so many people wanted to celebrate with dear Negussie that they had to move the wedding to a bigger church.

Negussie's smile was perhaps never bigger than on that wedding day. He carried himself with the regal dignity expected of Ethiopian grooms. And as ever, he had a childlike joy in God's provision for him.

Photo of Negussie and Fantaye at their wedding in Kenya.

Do you know that God designed weddings, and brides and grooms, to teach us something? In the Bible, God compares Jesus to a groom, and the church (all the people who put their faith in Jesus) to the bride. The Bible describes a day when all believers will see Jesus in heaven.

It's like a wedding day, full of beauty, celebration, and feasting. After so many years of waiting, Jesus—the one who loves us—will be with us forever. And we will enjoy his love and care for eternity in our new home.

After the years of waiting, Negussie and Fantaye's wedding was a beautiful reflection of God's design. They were finally united in joy.

Negussie and Fantaye at their home in Kenya.

The Finish Line

In his second year of study at the Bible college, Negussie wrote to John about his delight in married life. He was so happy to have Fantaye nearby. He loved the scent of his favorite spicy chicken stew, *doro wat*, that she cooked for him. He told John how grateful he was that God had given them a happy home and rest. In the cool evenings, after he had finished his schoolwork, Negussie would bring out his guitar and sing with Fantaye. As they worshiped the Lord together, she thanked God for answering her prayer for a godly husband.

In his third year of college, Negussie wrote another letter to John. He had been worried about his wife, who had not been feeling well. But soon they discovered the source of her sickness—Fantaye was expecting a baby! The year 1991 was going to be a year of new beginnings.

As Fantaye's body began growing the little life in her womb, new things were growing in Ethiopia as well. Other communist countries that had once supported Ethiopia were now falling apart and growing poorer themselves.

The foreign governments could no longer prop up the Ethiopian Derg. Across Ethiopia, people were suffering from the failed communist experiment. Famine, joblessness, homelessness, poverty, and lack of hope had devastated the country.

Communism finally ended in Ethiopia!

The revolution had not brought the transformation it had promised. Various rebel groups from across Ethiopia joined together to create their own army—The Ethiopian People's Revolutionary Democratic Front (EPRDF.) They began to fight together against the communist government, taking over city after city. As the army marched toward Addis Ababa, the statues of communist leaders were toppled over, and the red banners were torn down. Colonel Mengistu, the ruthless communist dictator, feared for his life after his brutal reign. So, he escaped the country in a small plane and went into hiding. In May of 1991, the EPRDF took control of Addis Ababa, and communist rule ended in Ethiopia.

The country soon opened for missionaries to return, and it did not take long for Murray and Bea Coleman to find their way back to Africa. When they returned, they were thrilled to visit Negussie and his beautiful bride.

Negussie and Fantaye watched the changes back home from the safety of their Kenyan apartment. Their hearts also yearned for the Ethiopian church. They dreamed about the days ahead. What would this newfound freedom for their homeland mean? Many people needed the hope and healing that only Jesus could bring after such terror and suffering.

In August of that year, they welcomed their beloved son, Nathanael. (Nathanael means "Gift of God," and indeed he was!) Soon after that, Pastor Kaydamo invited Negussie to do his college internship alongside him in Addis Ababa. Negussie and Fantaye returned to Ethiopia, where they introduced Fantaye's family to their firstborn son.

Negussie and Fantaye with their oldest son, Nathanael.

While they were away, Fantaye's family began to soften to Negussie and embrace their new family.

Meanwhile, over those five months back in Addis, Negussie served the church fervently. It had grown so large that it now had eleven congregations across the city! He wrote to John about the incredible work to be done in Ethiopia.

John and his wife, Phyllis, now with their sons Jeffrey and Nathan, were aware of the open door in Ethiopia. They were preparing to become missionaries there. Negussie was jubilant at the thought of serving alongside his best friend John. He imagined their wives enjoying a cup of tea and their sons playing together—perhaps climbing trees and looking for birds—just like John and Negussie had done as boys!

Then Negussie and Fantaye returned to Kenya for the last year of Bible school. They knew it would be an intense year of study. They also discovered that Fantaye was expecting another baby! Negussie worked toward the finish line of completing his studies. And as Fantaye neared the end of her pregnancy, things began to change once again.

God's Child

First, another handsome son was born. They named him "Nebeyu," which means "prophet." But then, Negussie seemed to be struggling more and more with his health. "It's just a cough," he'd say dismissively. But friends were concerned. They urged him to go to the Kijabe hospital in Nairobi.

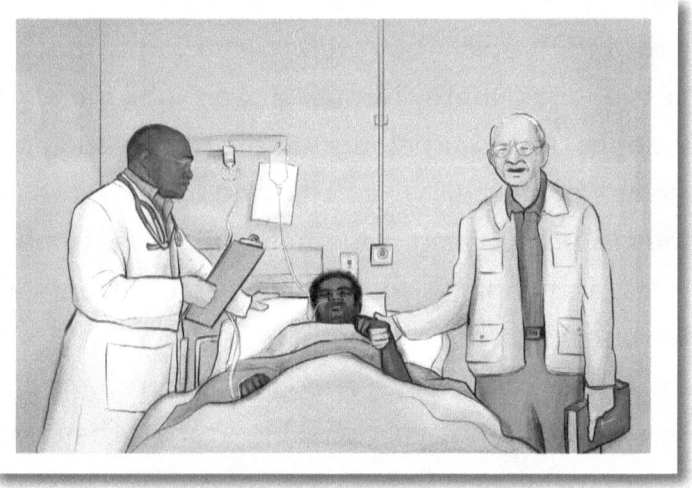

Negussie became very ill with typhoid.

At the hospital, Negussie received a diagnosis. He had an infectious fever called "typhoid." However, Negussie did not have time to slow down and get better. He had been busily completing his studies, and now he had to prepare his young family to move back to Ethiopia. Further, there was a new baby at home, and he took his role as father and husband seriously. He felt he couldn't stay any longer in the hospital, so he left.

Fantaye felt worry creep through her as she heard Negussie's coughing from the other room. He had returned from the hospital confident and cheerful, but she knew that he was not better. She stepped around the suitcases packed with their belongings and leaned on the doorframe. She spoke gently to her husband, hunched in his chair. "Perhaps we could stay in Kenya a little longer? You could take more classes here at Scott College." She wanted him to remain in Kenya where the medical help was more reliable and accessible.

He told her what she already knew. The scholarship money had run out, and it was too expensive for them to stay. Besides, he was so eager to begin ministry in Ethiopia during these fresh days of opportunity. And so, they flew home as scheduled.

But as the plane skipped and skidded to a halt upon arrival, Fantaye knew Negussie needed to be taken straight to the hospital. Fantaye called relatives to help her husband find the treatment he needed while she settled the little boys. Negussie spent the next few weeks transferring from clinic to clinic, in and out of hospitals.

News reached Bea and Murray about their dear Negussie. They hurried to find him at the hospital. He was visibly suffering, yet Negussie still greeted them with his usual friendliness. As they left the hospital room, they spoke in low, solemn voices to one another about how ill he looked.

The Colemans returned on Sunday to see Negussie again and to pray with him. They were cheered on this second visit, as it seemed that Negussie was doing much better! They felt hopeful that the worst was over for their dear son, Negussie, and promised to visit him again in a few weeks.

Before they returned to Addis, however, they received shocking news over the mission radio communications. Negussie had died. They were heartbroken. It all happened so quickly that they had even missed the funeral.

Paul and Lila Balisky had attended the funeral. They brought back notes from the service for the Colemans. At the funeral, Pastor Kaydamo counseled all who gathered to mourn the sudden loss of their dear friend and brother. He spoke from 2 Corinthians 5. He reminded them that our bodies are like tents. A tent wears out. We are not made to live in tents forever. If we put our faith in Jesus, our real home is built in heaven.

Pastor Kaydamo spoke at Negussie's funeral.

God's Child

Negussie's "tent" had grown weak, and it was time for him to join his beloved Lord Jesus in his forever home in heaven. Negussie was happy with God! But Pastor Kaydamo admitted that he was very sad. Why had God allowed Negussie, who was only 41, to die when Pastor Kaydamo was well into his 60s? Imagine all the work Negussie could have done in their church! But they could all take courage. All through prison and beatings and illness, Negussie had bravely hoped in his heavenly home. And now he was there! And one day, all who trust in Jesus will join Negussie and Jesus in their heavenly home.

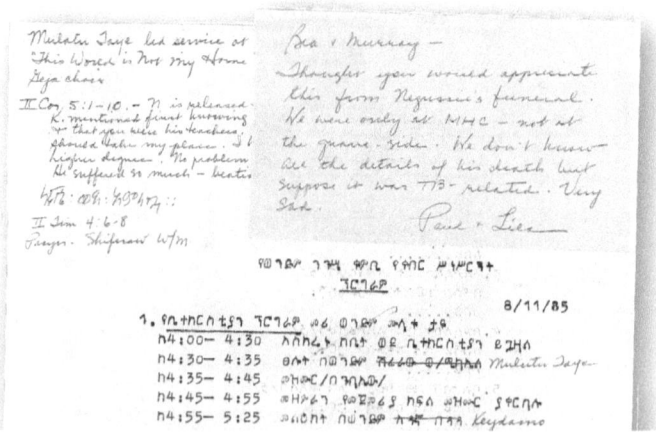

Paul and Lila gave notes from the funeral to the Colemans.

Fantaye's family arranged to have Negussie buried and gave him a beautiful gravesite. Carved into arched gray stone are a cross and an open Bible—the two things Negussie had based his whole life upon. Fantaye chose a verse to be engraved on the stone:

Then, when our dying bodies have been transformed into bodies that will never die, this [promise] will be fulfilled:

"Death is swallowed up in victory.

O death, where is your victory?

O death, where is your sting?"
(1 Corinthians 15:54–55 NLT)

Fantaye had a long road ahead of her. Her husband was buried, and his spirit was away from her and with the Lord Jesus. She was now alone to raise her two beautiful boys. But she consoled herself with the knowledge that Negussie's broken body would be transformed into a perfect, heavenly one. She trusted that one day death would no longer sting her heart the way it did now.

Fantaye's family gave Negussie a beautiful grave.

You see, when you put your faith in Jesus to be your Lord and Savior, he gives you eternal life. That means you will live forever with him. After you die, your body will die, but your soul will live forever. Then, one day, Jesus is going to raise up all people who have believed in him. We will be given new, heavenly bodies that cannot get sick or hurt or die. Death will not win. Jesus will have the victory. Death will not sting our hearts, and we will have peace and joy forever with God.

I know this is a sad story. I know that you, like so many others, have grown to care about Negussie from hearing his story. But I tell you this story because it is true, and because there are so many important things you and I can learn from Negussie.

The first is that you must ask yourself if you are God's child. All the courage and hope and joy that Negussie had throughout his life came because he trusted in Jesus as his Savior and Lord. He did not need to be afraid of anything—even death—because he was God's child. Negussie is safe and loved and whole in the presence of his heavenly Father right now.

Second, we can learn from Negussie's promise to John in his 1974 letter. He wanted to be a light for Jesus anywhere—wherever God would send him. You see, Negussie had been working hard to go to Bible college to become a pastor. But we can see that he was serving Jesus all along the way. He did not need to finish his degree to begin ministry. He had shown others the way to Jesus by his obedient life. He shared the gospel at every opportunity he had—even as a young boy whom Nurse Ott asked to teach the little kids' Sunday school class! Children do not need to wait to be a light for Jesus. You can obey him and follow him today and every day.

We don't know how long our lives will be. John wrote to Murray and Bea after hearing about Negussie's death. In his letter he wondered why God allows some to die young and others to live a long time. In the Bible, Peter and James were in prison together—James was killed, but Peter went free. John the Baptist's life was cut short by a cruel king, but the apostle John lived to be 90 years old. He served the Lord through old age.

In the same way, Negussie had died too soon for all the people who loved him on this earth. But John Coleman would spend the next few decades with his family serving the Lord in Ethiopia. We do not know how long we will have. But we can live each day for God.

Epilogue

John and Phyllis and their children served in Ethiopia, working with pregnant women and orphaned children for many years. From among those babies, they adopted two daughters for themselves, twins they named Abby and Amy. Abby means "a father's joy" and Amy means "beloved." Also, from among those orphaned babies, Fantaye adopted a daughter, whom she named Fikir, which means "love" in Amharic.

John and his family continued to serve in Ethiopia.

Like Negussie was welcomed into the Coleman home, more Ethiopian children were adopted and welcomed into families. Adoption is another way God shows his love for us. It is a picture of how we can become God's children, welcomed into our heavenly Father's family.

Fantaye chose to follow Jesus faithfully. She raised her children to know and love Jesus, to read the Bible and pray. At age three, Fantaye changed her second son's name from "Nebeyu" to "Mikiyas." It means, "There is no one like God." It was a way to show that after all she had been through, she was still holding fast to her faith in Jesus. There was no one like her faithful God who had met her in her sorrow and carried her along.

As I write this book, both of Negussie's sons have completed school. They serve in their churches—Nathanael is a worship pastor, and Mikiyas teaches classes for new believers at his church. Both sons have found wives who love Jesus, and Nathanael has welcomed a son into his family.

Epilogue

As John Coleman, who called Fantaye for an update, wrote to me at the end of his email: "They have trusted the Lord and found him faithful." May we do the same!

Negussie wrote many letters during his life.

Acknowledgments

To my husband Sean, who is the greatest teammate and my favorite person, thank you. You make it possible for me to work at things I love and also be a wife and mom. I'm so grateful for the load you carry to make it happen.

To Vivian and the team at William Carey Publishing, thank you for your patience with a rookie like me and your eagerness to teach children about missions.

To Kay Bascom, whose book *Hidden Triumph in Ethiopia* sparked the idea of telling this story to children and paved the way to do so. Your enthusiastic encouragement, keen advice, and fervent prayers gave fuel to this fire when I was growing dim. Thank you for putting your lamp on a stand to give light to all and bring glory to our heavenly Father.

To Fantaye, I have such deep appreciation for you, my sister, and I look forward to meeting you someday. Thank you for choosing Jesus day after day, no matter how hard it may be.

I am forever grateful for the help and support of John and Phyllis Coleman, who provided me with folders of notes and photographs and a pile of John's letters from Negussie (which were invaluable for me to see the heart of this dear man). You added to that an excellent stack of books from Murray's and your own library so I could learn more about Ethiopia, the work of SIM, and the Red Terror. From helping me decipher Amharic writing, to letting me hold the hat Negussie wove for John, to calling Fantaye for updates, you've walked alongside me to make this project happen—you gave me the precious resources I needed. And by extension, to Bea, your care in preserving this story made it possible for me to tell it a generation later and half a world away. Thank you for loving Jesus, Negussie, and Ethiopia.

To Jessica, Marina, and Courtney, you are my dear co-laborers in the gospel. Thank you for helping me in our wonderful and difficult work and praying often for this project (and for making me laugh so much along the way).

Acknowledgments

To the children of Hillsdale, who let me tell you stories and speak of my wonderful Lord—thank you for listening. I know you fell in love with Negussie as we went through this story together, and I pray you will live faithfully as he did, no matter what you face in the days ahead.

Introducing Mission Kids, a new collection from William Carey Publishing. These books are designed for young readers to nurture a passion for the peoples of the world and inspire them to participate in God's global mission.

Perfect Peace Child: A True Story of How One Tribe Found Forever Peace

Steve Richardson with **Maxine McDonald**
Illustrated by Sarah Nunnally

Journey by canoe into the jungles of New Guinea and discover a colorful village hidden high in the trees.

Perfect Peace Child tells the true story of how God used the Sawi people's own tradition—giving a baby to make peace—to show them that Jesus is God's Peace Child. That's when their hearts began to change.

This book invites children to see how God's love brings deep-down-forever peace anywhere in the world.

www.ingramcontent.com/pod-product-compliance
Lightning Source LLC
Chambersburg PA
CBHW030556080526
44585CB00012B/387